# A $25,000 PASSIVE INCOME INVESTMENT

CASE STUDY AND WORKBOOK

# A $25,000 PASSIVE INCOME INVESTMENT

Alexis S. Assadi

# Disclaimer

Although a reasonable person would understand that I'm sharing my personal experiences with you – not advising you on how to conduct yours – there are some people who don't take responsibility for their own actions. What they'd instead prefer to do is to take this case study and try to find a way to sue me for what's in it. It happens all the time (thankfully not yet to me, but there's always a first!).

As you know, I'm neither a lawyer nor a financial advisor. In fact, I'm not any kind of licensed professional. I didn't even get a driver's license until I was 25. So don't rely on the information herein to make your business/investment/ life decisions. For all you know, everything I said in this case study could be completely wrong. It could all be a massive lie conjured up by darker forces bent on world domination by spreading disinformation.

Instead, what I think you should do is to use what's in here as a piece of your business/investment puzzle. Take what you find to be useful and use it however you please. Some people try to protect themselves by saying "this case study was for entertainment purposes only." I have a bit more dignity than that, so please just be reasonable and use at your own risk.

PS – I made up the company, BC Ice Rinks Ltd. To my knowledge, it does not exist. However, if it in fact does, all references made to BIR are coincidental and bear no truth about it. I'm also not recommending that you lend money to or invest in BC Ice Rinks Ltd.

# TABLE OF CONTENTS

SECTION 1

# INTRODUCTION

Most of the investments I make are ones that produce instant passive income, preferably paid monthly, or ones that at least have a strong potential to do so. In this case study, I share with you the particulars of a $25,000 investment that I made into a small business in British Columbia, Canada, in 2015.

Here, I explain how the opportunity came about and what **due diligence** (research) I performed prior to moving forward with it. In the various exhibits I disclose the legal and corporate documents that were used to execute the investment, as well as how and why it was structured in the way it was. You will see the risks that I took on and how I sought to manage them. I also discuss some of the distinct realities of doing business with an entrepreneur and how these realities need to be considered in such a deal.

It is important to note that this case study is not intended to show you how I became financially free or what broad business and investing principles I employ. Many of those are available in my book, Rich At 26. Instead, here you will discover the minutiae that's involved in my investments; things like corporations, interest rates, lawyers, relationships and more. You will find that the deals I do are unlike trading stocks or purchasing assets that are traditionally recommended by financial advisors. They require not only calculation, but also a combination of common sense, problem solving, creativity and a spirit of partnership.

Although all of the information in this case study is true, for privacy purposes, I have changed and/or redacted some names and confidential details.

## Learning Objectives

**1** Learn to make investments that benefit the investor, entrepreneur and customer

**2** Identify the pros and cons of equity and debt financing

**3** Draft a contract that protects the investor's interests

**4** Understand what a corporation is and how an investor can bypass its shield

**5** Perform due diligence to assess the risks associated with an investment

**6** Mitigate the risks discovered in the due diligence process

**7** Formulate an exit strategy to recoup an investment

**8** Balance personal relationships with financial interests

**9** Apply this case study to your own personal investments

SECTION 2

# HOW I FOUND THIS INVESTMENT

If you have read Rich At 26, you already know that building relationships and making connections was a big part of how I became financially free. Establishing a wide network of entrepreneurs and investors opened up a stream of investment opportunities – some better than others – that I've capitalized on.

The example in this case study was no different. I made this investment with a former colleague, Dave, with whom I once worked with as a salesperson until he quit the job in 2011. Dave had decided that he would pursue a path of entrepreneurship rather than remaining an employee. His plan to escape the rat race was to assemble real estate deals, finance them by raising money from investors, manage the

NOTES

properties himself and then keep a portion of the profits generated from them.

For instance, Dave might use investors' money to buy a $250,000 house. After purchasing the real estate, he would then manage, renovate and rent it to tenants with the aim of increasing its value over time. While the investors would contribute capital to the deal, Dave would supply effort (often called "sweat equity"). Thus, in exchange for his work, he would retain a portion (30-50%) of the profits from the investment.

Such a strategy would provide Dave with an ownership stake in potentially dozens of pieces of real estate, without having to use any of his own funds. It would be a win-win scenario: Dave's clients would receive access to property investments and, in return, he would be paid a performance fee. At the time, the concept seemed ingenious to me but highly risky. I was interested to see where his journey would lead and we kept in touch after his departure. We frequently traded emails, saw each other at conferences and had several mutual friends and associates.

NOTES

About a year later, Dave approached me for an investment. But instead of pitching a real estate deal, he asked me for a loan to help fund his general business. He explained that in the past several months his clientele had grown tremendously. There was a pent-up demand for the service that Dave provided because people increasingly wanted access to passive real estate opportunities. Rather than simply operating as "Dave," he now wanted to start a formal company, move into an office and begin advertising on social media. He felt that a $25,000 injection of cash would accelerate the business and wondered whether I would lend it to him.

To make it worth my while, Dave offered me an interest rate of 15% per year. In exchange for $25,000, he would pay me $312.50 in interest on the first day of each month until he returned the principal amount (the amount loaned). In one year I would therefore earn $3,750 in interest. Although it was a loan, it would still technically be an investment; one that would pay 15% in annual passive income.

NOTES

**LEARNING POINT** Investments into businesses are commonly structured as loans. These are called "debt investments." A purchase of shares in a business, however, is called an "equity investment."

While the deal seemed both simple and lucrative, I had never done anything similar to it before. I was also 24 years old and didn't have $25,000. I had only recently graduated from university and was still paying off debts. Regardless, I decided to take the plunge. The chance to earn a passive income of over $300 a month seemed too good to pass up. I told Dave that I would find the cash and committed to making the investment with him.

The extent of my due diligence was to seek the advice of two friends, who at the time were law and accounting students. While they had no experience in the field, they still did their best to help me understand the details of the deal. Since I had almost no cash, my then-girlfriend let me borrow from her student line of credit, which I in turn loaned to Dave. My girlfriend paid the bank an interest rate of 3%, I paid her 8% and Dave paid me

NOTES

15%. So she made an annual 5% profit, I made 7% and Dave got to finance his business – all by using the bank's funds.

That was my first time investing with Dave. Although we were both amateurs and I was lucky to not lose the money, the deal was a success and we continued doing business together. It was the beginning of what would later become a lucrative partnership. In the following years, Dave kept offering good investments from which we both profited. They were not only fruitful economically, but they taught me a great deal about finance, business and investing with entrepreneurs. By participating in them, I learned how to structure deals, better manage risk and read and understand contracts.

Of course, every relationship experiences its pitfalls. In spite of our relative prosperity, there was one project that soured. In 2013 Dave approached me to invest into his latest venture, a marketing company. Although it was again an "out of the box" opportunity, I trusted him enough to move forward with it. Shortly after buying my shares in the business, though, Dave found another partner who was willing to invest the same amount but

NOTES

for less ownership in it. Despite our contract, he returned my capital without interest and kicked me out of the deal altogether. I chose to not challenge him because I felt that attempting to enforce our agreement would not be worth the costs or the harm to our partnership. After all, I did not lose any money. As I write this (February 2016), Dave is now listing the company for sale and my decision to back down thus cost me several thousand dollars in potential profits. At the time, I felt that what he did was bad business and it left a sour taste in my mouth for several months.

Nonetheless, I came to understand Dave's logic. It was a business decision, not personal, and I was still impressed by his ability to build a full-scale marketing firm. The damage done wasn't enough to cause me to end our dealings together. In the following years I watched him construct a substantial portfolio of companies and properties, all by using other people's money and generating returns on it for them. Whether through land developments, rentals, flips or business acquisitions, Dave had a knack for putting cash into his clients' pockets, including mine, time and time again. He gained

NOTES

local notoriety as one of the town's premier entrepreneurs. So in the summer of 2015, when he approached me for another $25,000 loan, it didn't take much for me to accept his offer

**LEARNING POINT** Although networking is important, sometimes successful entrepreneurs are met through the regular course of life. Don't discount connections that you didn't actively seek. Meeting someone through a friend or through your job is no less valuable than doing so by attending a function or an investment/entrepreneurship event.

NOTES

SECTION 3

# THE DEAL

This time, Dave's request was actually on behalf of his wife, Laura, who operated an ice skating rink in British Columbia (we'll call it BC Ice Rinks Ltd., or BIR). Her business was well-established and earned annual profits of $60,000, but to maximize its revenue she wanted to add a series of vending machines that she could then charge her customers to use. Rather than paying the fixed costs of additional employees, she wanted to have an asset that would produce income at – literally – the push of a button.

Laura's plan was for BIR to borrow cash from me and to then use it to purchase the vending machines. The business would pay 12% interest per year on the loan and would repay the money through the sales that it harvested from its new assets. She projected

NOTES

that, once installed, the machines would generate an income of $1,400 per month. If successful, BIR would acquire revenue-creating equipment that was purchased with my capital and paid for by Laura's customers. In exchange, the customers would receive inexpensive, on-demand snacks and drinks and I would earn $250 per month from BIR's interest payments (a 12% annual return on $25,000, paid monthly), which would be pure passive income. Just like Dave's deals, this one would benefit the company, the clients and me. It was exactly the type of investment that I like to make.

- BIR borrows $25,000 from me at an interest rate of 12% per year. Interest payments are made monthly.
- BIR then uses that money to buy vending machines.
- After installing the equipment, BIR can potentially generate an extra $1,400 of monthly income.
- The income generated from those sales would be used to repay my loan with interest.
- The loan must be repaid within two years.

NOTES

While 12% interest is not an unreasonable borrowing rate, you may perhaps wonder why Laura would pay that much for a loan. Why not approach the bank and get money for, say, 6%? Why would she use a private investor like me and pay twice as much for capital?

Unfortunately, at that time, it had only been eight months since Laura incorporated BIR. For years prior she had operated her ice rink as a sole proprietorship, which meant that it was simply an extension of herself. Even though it had separate bank accounts and a business license, the company was legally still "Laura." By incorporating it, however, BIR became a separate legal entity with its own rights, powers, credit history and net worth. In fact, in the eyes of the law, a corporation is similar to a person. As such, just like a bank requires proof of income and adequate credit from a person before lending to her/him, it requests the same from a corporation. But since BC Ice Rinks Ltd. was only recently incepted, it had no credit history and only eight months of revenue. Thus, it could not qualify for a loan. From the bank's perspective, Laura's business had only just begun.

NOTES

**LEARNING POINT** In the eyes of the law, a corporation is its own "person."

Many entrepreneurs face the same challenge that Laura did. Most banks have stringent restrictions when lending to small business owners and will require extensive financial histories and/or substantial collateral before extending credit to them. As a result, fledgling companies often cannot secure the financing they need to grow and frequently fail because of that.

Unable to obtain debt from a bank, Laura's other options were to raise capital by selling shares in her company (raising equity), or to borrow from a private investor who would look beyond the hazards that traditional lenders perceived. Choosing between the two, debt verses equity, is another dilemma that entrepreneurs commonly encounter.

By selling shares to investors, Laura would not have had to repay the money if the business failed. As shareholders, the investors would be owners of the company, not lenders, and would not be entitled to recourse. In that respect, raising equity comes with

NOTES

less risk. However, doing so would also have caused Laura to lose a degree of ownership and control of BIR. For instance, if she owned 100 out of 100 shares in the firm, but to raise capital sold 25 of them for $1,000 per share ($25,000), Laura would then only own 75% of the company. While she would still control it (since she owned over 50%), 25% of BIR's profits would be allocated to the other investors.

As such, when deciding whether to raise equity or debt, Laura probably calculated that the cost of losing total ownership and sharing profits with others would be greater than the cost of borrowing money. Thus, she opted to secure debt financing. But in exchange for ease, flexibility and a tolerance for risk that banks would not stomach, BIR would have to pay a higher interest rate on the loan.

**LEARNING POINT** Debt (borrowing money) and equity (selling shares for money) financing each come with their own benefits and downsides.

NOTES

After hearing the pitch from Dave, I thought that Laura's strategy for BIR made sense. The company would buy the vending machines, install them and begin producing fresh revenue streams almost overnight. Since they would be located in a popular ice rink with plenty of customers, I believed that the machines would probably generate the projected $1,400 in monthly income fairly quickly. In two years, that would amount to $33,600, which would be more than enough to cover the $31,000 debt owed to me ($25,000 principal and $6,000 interest over two years). There would also be a $2,600 margin of error. With a reasonable cash buffer and knowing that BIR already earned a monthly profit of $5,000, the risk appeared to be quite low. Even if the vending machines foundered, the company could likely repay me from its existing earnings.

However, while I felt that Laura's action plan was astute and was satisfied by the potential return on investment (ROI), I had similar concerns as the banks, but for different reasons. Unlike the banks, I didn't mind that BIR lacked an established financial

NOTES

history because I understood that incorporating it was an administrative activity. Her business did have profits. Instead, I wasn't comfortable with lending funds to a corporation.

- BIR owes me $25,000 in principal and $6,000 in interest, totalling $31,000.
- The vending machines should produce $1,400 per month, or $33,600 over the term of the loan.
- If Laura's projections are accurate, the vending machines will produce $2,600 more than what is required to repay my loan, leaving a reasonable buffer to help cover any shortfalls in revenue.
- BIR already produced an annual profit of $60,000, which it could use to pay me if the vending machines failed.

NOTES

## The Corporate Veil

Just like a person, a corporation can borrow money. However, since it is a separate and distinct entity from its owners, a corporation can (break a contractual obligation) on its debts without its shareholders, directors, officers or employees incurring any liability. That meant that if I loaned capital to BIR – not to Laura personally – and the company collapsed, I could lose my money and she legally would not have to repay me. My cash would die along with her business, and she could escape unscathed.

The veil of a corporation exists to protect its owners and employees. That's why when a business is sued, it is frequently the corporation that is named as the defendant and not its staff. Even if individuals are named in the suit, they are often dropped from it after it is demonstrated that the corporate shield protects them from liability. For example, when several US banks were sued for triggering the 2008 economic recession, the companies, not their employees, paid millions of dollars in penalties and settlement costs. Another clear-cut example is

NOTES

if a corporation owes credit card debt, it, not its employees, is responsible to pay it.

A corporation is a necessary tool for a lot of businesspeople. I have a few of them, myself, to ensure that my assets are safe. Even my blog (AlexisAssadi.net) is owned by a company, Assadi Global Ventures, Inc., and not by me. Although I may personally benefit from the website, I may be able to share any liability for the content posted on it with that company.

Although discussions about lawsuits may seem a bit dark, they are a reality that need to be addressed. The more successful you are, the more exposed you become, so it is important to protect yourself legally. Or as one of my friends says, "C.Y.A." – Cover Your Ass. One of the ways to do that is by incorporating, which can protect your business assets not only from yourself, but also from other businesses or investments that you own. Many people, for instance, use a different corporation for each piece of real estate that they buy. If one property is sued or foreclosed upon, a correct structure can prevent the others from being impacted.

NOTES ______________________________

______________________________

______________________________

______________________________

______________________________

______________________________

______________________________

**LEARNING POINT** Depending on where you live, corporations can make your investments and businesses either more or less tax efficient. Be sure to consider your asset protection strategies along with their tax implications.

Since corporations can provide shelter to investors and entrepreneurs, they can pose an obstacle to lenders. Usually, unless there's evidence of wrongdoing, it is hard to force a person to repay a corporation's debts. Sometimes companies fail and simply can't pay back the money they owe; there's nothing fraudulent about that, it's just the nature of business.

While I wanted to invest in Laura's company, I was also unwilling to release her of personal liability. In spite of my relationship with Dave and my faith in their ability to build successful ventures, if BIR was to receive a loan from me, I needed Laura to be bound to it, too. As such, I sought to **bypass the corporate shield.**

NOTES

To do so, I would require Laura to sign a **personal guarantee** (Exhibit D). That guarantee meant that even if her company defaulted on the debt, she would be responsible for repaying it. It is essentially akin to lending the money to her personally. Unless she went bankrupt and lost all of her assets, Laura would have to pay me back regardless. Even if she died, her estate would still owe me the money. Only a guarantee would afford me the comfort I needed to lend to BIR. She agreed, reluctantly, to incur the personal liability so that I would make the investment.

**LEARNING POINT** Try to get a personal guarantee when lending to a corporation.

It should be noted that there are often rules that govern the usage of personal guarantees. People often co-sign for loans without cognizance of what the implications of doing so are. Therefore, in places like Alberta, Canada, a person cannot guarantee a loan without the oversight of a lawyer. If it is done without one, the guarantee may be unenforceable.

NOTES ______

## Execution

My investment into BIR was thus executed through the use of two legally-binding documents. The first was a loan agreement, which facilitated a loan from my investment company (I usually invest through corporations instead of doing so personally) to Laura's business. As demonstrated in Exhibit C, the loan agreement stated all of the terms and conditions of the arrangement, including the amount loaned, the interest rate and the maturity date (when BIR needed to repay the loan).

**LEARNING POINT** A loan agreement is a contract where one party (the lender) promises to lend money, and the receiving party (the borrower) pledges to repay it. It is the basis of any debt financing investment.

In some cases, investors prefer to use a **promissory note**, rather than a loan agreement, to document an indebtedness. The primary difference between the two is that a promissory note only needs to be signed by the borrower and not by the lender. Oftentimes both are used in support of each other.

NOTES

I employ loan agreements, though, not promissory notes, simply out of personal preference.

In addition to the loan agreement, the second contract was the personal guarantee, which we called a "Letter of Guarantee." Although it is a lengthy read, it essentially said: "I, Laura, promise to make sure that BIR repays its loan to Alexis' investment company. If it doesn't, then I will repay it."

- To facilitate the loan from my company to BIR, we used a Loan Agreement
- To bypass the corporate veil and bind Laura to the loan, we used a Letter of Guarantee

Since BIR, Laura and I were located in different cities, the agreements were executed electronically. Laura signed her portions in front of a witness and emailed a scanned copy to me for my execution. After I signed and returned it to her, the contracts were considered complete and I advanced the funds to BIR. We then mailed the original documents to one another, but that was largely a formality.

NOTES

**LEARNING POINT** Both parties should sign the contracts in front of a witness.

As with any contract, a loan agreement and personal guarantee are binding under the law. There are serious implications if either party reneges on its obligations. The loan agreement compelled my firm to lend money to BIR on a certain date. Thereafter, BIR had several responsibilities, including making monthly interest payments at a rate of 12% per annum and returning the capital to me in 24 months.

If BIR contravened the contract, such as failing to make timely payments, I would have had several options for recourse. These included:

- Renegotiating the loan agreement and increasing the interest rate
- Renegotiating the loan agreement and including fees and penalties
- Recalling the loan and demanding immediate repayment of it

NOTES

If a satisfactory resolution could not be reached, my final option would have been to file a civil lawsuit in court. The defendant would not only have been BIR, but also the guarantor, Laura. If the suit was successful I would have received a **judgment** against them, which is a court order demanding that the loan be repaid. If the judgment was not abided by, I could then have proceeded to place a **lien** (a security interest that prevents the borrower from realizing profits on a sale until the debt is repaid) on their assets, seize bank accounts and garnish wages in order to recoup my capital.

Note that the exit strategy in this investment depended heavily on BIR and Laura's willingness and ability to repay me. Unlike an equity deal, though, it did not require a **liquidity event** such as an acquisition or a listing on the stock market. Instead, the firm just needed to make enough money to be able to pay me back. If the loan agreement was followed, then I would have had no issue in recovering the loan. At the time of writing, my investment into BIR is only six months old so I have not yet exited from it.

NOTES

I will discuss an alternative exit strategy later on in this case study.

**LEARNING POINT** Stockholders in privately-held companies typically exit by selling their shares to another buyer. That often means being bought out buy a larger company or taking the firm public.

NOTES

SECTION 4

# THE CONTRACTS

Loan agreements and letters of guarantee are standard documents. A lawyer can draft them with ease. For these types of deals, though, I prefer to write the contracts myself. I have made dozens of debt investments in recent years and am quite familiar with what is required. In fact, there is often little variation between the agreements. After drafting one, I simply send it to my lawyer for his comments. He reviews it, makes amendments and then returns it to me. That reduces the legal fees involved in the transaction.

NOTES

## Fees

You will notice that Section 13 of the loan agreement stipulated that BIR had to reimburse me for my legal fees, as well as for all other reasonable costs that I incurred throughout the course of the deal. For instance, if I had to hire a collection agency to help enforce the loan or if my bank charged me transaction fees, the company would have to repay me for them. The letter of guarantee made Laura liable for those costs, too.

To some, that might perhaps appear to be one-sided or unfair. After all, why did BIR have to pay my bills? Shouldn't each party have been responsible for its own costs? While that may seem reasonable at face value, it is actually crucial for a lender to require reimbursement from the borrower for the following reasons:

First, if BIR defaulted on the loan and I was forced to litigate to recover it, the costs to do so could have been high. I would likely have had to issue demand letters through registered mail, file a claim in court and hire a lawyer to pursue the debt. That could have easily cost $10,000. Considering that the

NOTES

entire deal was for $25,000 and my total profit from it was $6,000, those fees would have expunged my returns completely.

Depending on the jurisdiction, a $31,000 lawsuit could be filed in Small Claims Court. Such arenas are used for modest civil claims and the parties typically represent themselves instead of hiring attorneys. That way one can avoid the high cost of legal bills. However, there is not enough margin in small investments to afford losing any amount of money. Therefore, such costs should be reimbursed. Where I live, Small Claims Court only hears claims of up to $25,000, so I would have had to file suit in the Provincial Court and would have likely needed legal counsel.

Second, with the above in mind, BIR could have purposely refused to repay all or some of the loan, calculating that it wouldn't be worth my cost of litigation to pursue it. For instance, if it repaid $30,000 out of $31,000, would I spend the money to recover the outstanding $1,000? Would it not be easier and cheaper to cut my losses? In some jurisdictions this is of lesser concern because the court might automatically award costs to the lender,

NOTES

regardless of whether it is stated in the agreement. But, to avoid potential loopholes, my contracts always specifically require borrowers to reimburse me. I've even seen agreements where the borrower has to pay interest on any fees incurred by the lender.

For this particular investment, I charged BIR an up-front fee of $131.25. My lawyer had advised me ahead of time how much he would bill to review the loan agreement and letter of guarantee, so I included the amount in the contract.

To collect fees or reimbursements, I do not issue invoices and expect a separate payment of them. Instead, I simply apply the borrower's monthly payments against the interest and fees owed before applying them to the principal (see Section 10 of the loan agreement). For example, if in one month BIR made a payment of $1,000, it would have been applied in the following order:

- $250 to interest
- $131.25 to fees
- $618.75 to principal

NOTES ______________________________

In one previous deal, however, I deducted my legal fees from the amount of the loan. In 2014 I issued credit for $106,000, but since I paid $6,000 in legal fees to do so, I only advanced $100,000 to the borrower. He still paid interest on $106,000, though.

While there are several ways to structure and fund a loan, in general, my preference is to add fees to the debt instead of subtracting them from it. If I have to litigate, I would feel more comfortable showing the judge that I deposited the amount stated in the loan agreement. In the above example, the borrower might have argued that he only ever received $100,000, not $106,000, and should therefore only be liable for that amount. Though I've been advised that such an argument would not hold water, I nonetheless prefer to avoid that scenario.

**LEARNING POINT** The Borrower should reimburse you for any reasonable costs that you incur over the course of the investment.

NOTES

## Profiting From Fees

Although the fee that I charged to BIR was simply to cover my legal costs, many lenders build them in as an additional profit center. It is not uncommon to include "administration" or "processing" or "set-up" fees that amount to 3-5% of the principal sum. There are also "early repayment" fees in case the borrower pays back the loan ahead of the maturity date. Depending on the jurisdiction, fees can usually be as high as the lender desires, so long as they do not push the **effective interest rate** on the loan high enough violate the **usury law** (which sets the maximum interest that can be legally charged).

For example, I could have charged BIR an administration fee of $2,000 (8% of $25,000). That cost would have increased the effective interest rate to around 17% per annum, which is well below what a lender can charge in my local province. As you will notice in Section 12 of the loan agreement, if the usury rate decreased during the term of the loan, the interest that I charged would automatically fall, too. That way I was prevented from inadvertently charging above what is allowed under law. For

NOTES

instance, if BIR had to pay a $2,000 administration fee and the usury rate then fell to 10%, the interest would have been adjusted accordingly.

**LEARNING POINT** Be aware of usury laws. Charging too much interest can be a criminal offense.

Out of preference, I typically do not include set-up fees in my loans beyond what is required to cover my costs. I consider them an underhanded way to mask a higher interest rate. However, I do take an aggressive approach to ensuring that monthly payments are made on time. Borrowers are often late with their payments, which ultimately threatens the safety of a lender's capital.

The loan agreement with BIR required it to make payments to my company on the first day of each month. While I didn't include this provision in the deal, I will often add a **late payment penalty** of 1% of the loan amount to ensure that they are made punctually. As such, if BIR was to make a payment even a single day late, it would be charged a $250

NOTES

fee. I will also include additional penalties for any cheques that bounce (these are often called **NSF** [non-sufficient funds] **fees**).

In my view, adding fees to a deal is a fair exchange of commerce. If a borrower makes his payments on time, I then have an easy-to-manage, passive investment. However, if he is late, I may have to spend resources to contact and remind him to make the payment. It can also become quite stressful. As such, I should be compensated for my efforts. Late fees incentivise the borrower to be punctual, thus providing me with a passive income stream. They do not *force* him to pay extra in fees; he will only do so if he does not keep his contractual obligation to make timely payments.

**LEARNING POINT** Fees not only encourage timely payments, but they can also be a substantial profit center.

NOTES

## Lawyers

Lawyers can be a crucial component to making investments. While they are useful to ensure that your ventures are legally sound, they can also assist with due diligence by finding potential faults in a deal. In my experience, their analytical skills are helpful. I, personally, consult with counsel prior to signing any kind of agreement. The cost of a good attorney can be well worth the risks you could face without one.

A mistake that many people make, however, is to *rely* on legal counsel for their contracts. I have worked with various lawyers over the years, some of whom are supposedly "the best" in their respective fields, and I have yet to come across one who did his job perfectly. Each agreement, without fail, that I have had an attorney draft has had an error in it. Sometimes they are as small as a spelling omission, but at other times they have been material (substantial or impactful). I even hired one who misstated my investment amount by $54,000!

NOTES

Regardless of an attorney's abilities, when it comes to contracts, it is imperative that you check over his work. A contract is what comprises the foundation of an investment. The slightest mistake can put both you and your capital at risk. You should be able to understand each clause of every agreement that you sign. Don't simply assume that your lawyers are prudent. As a rule of thumb, remember this: you are responsible for your own business; nobody will ever care about it as much as you do.

**LEARNING POINT**

Always double-check your lawyer's work.

## Notable Sections in the Loan Agreement

Every loan agreement is different, depending on the parties' preferences and the nature of the transaction. However, I would like to underscore a few specific sections in the one that I used for this deal:

NOTES

## Section 9: Governing Law

This Loan Agreement and all acts and transactions pursuant hereto and the rights and obligations of the parties hereto shall be governed, construed and interpreted in accordance with the laws of the Province of British Columbia, without giving effect to principles of conflicts of law, and the parties will attorn themselves to the jurisdiction of the courts in the City of .

As mentioned, both BIR and Laura were located in a different city from me, about a 10 hour drive away. If there was a disagreement over the deal and we had to go to court to resolve it, I wanted to do it where I lived and not have to take an airplane to get there. This clause stated that the terms of the loan agreement would be governed by the laws in my local jurisdiction. In the event of litigation, we would go to court in my city, not theirs. As a result, it would help reduce the up-front costs that I would incur by travelling (flights, hotels, etc.). It would also make it harder for BIR and Laura to defend themselves by increasing their expenses.

NOTES

**LEARNING POINT** Specify where you want legal action to take place. If you don't, the court will decide for you.

### Section 16: Independent Legal Advice

The Borrower and the Lender acknowledge and agree that each party has had the opportunity to seek independent legal advice with respect to the subject matter of this Agreement.

The Borrower acknowledges and agrees that it has sought independent legal advice or waives such advice. (Borrower's initials).

People sometimes argue that they were duped into signing a contract, that they were improperly advised to do so or that they did not understand what they were signing. To help prevent against that, I ensured that Laura formally acknowledged (and initialed next to it) that she had sought independent legal advice, or that she waived her opportunity to do so.

**LEARNING POINT** Have the other party initial next to any part(s) of the contract that are particularly important.

NOTES

## Section 17: Counterpart Execution

This Agreement may be executed in counterpart and delivered via electronic email in scanned document format and together such counterparts shall be deemed to constitute a single original.

This clause stated that the parties could sign the loan agreement over email, rather than having to meet in-person to do so. Since there was a lot of distance between Laura and I, this section was particularly useful.

## Section 22: Entire Agreement

This Agreement constitutes the entire agreement between the Borrower and the Lender, and supersedes all prior agreements and understandings, oral or written, by and between the Borrower and the Lender with respect to the subject matter hereof.

In my opinion, the "Entire Agreement" clause is one of the most valuable components of a contract. It essentially stated that only the content of the agreement was binding upon the parties. People will often try to shimmy out of deals by arguing that something else was agreed upon, too, but it just

NOTES ______________________________

wasn't put into writing. This final section said, "No. Everything we agreed upon is what was written in here." It is for everyone's protection.

### Section 8: Transfer, Successors and Assigns

The terms and conditions of this Agreement shall enure to the benefit of and be binding upon the respective successors and assigns of the Borrower. The Lender may assign, pledge, or otherwise transfer this Agreement without the prior consent of the Borrower. This Agreement may be transferred only upon surrender of the original Agreement, accompanied by a duly executed written instrument of transfer in form satisfactory to the Borrower and the transferee.

Loan agreements and personal guarantees are assets and can therefore be sold. This clause underscored that point. For example, if a person sought an income producing investment, I could have sold him the rights to this $25,000 loan to BIR for $26,000 (or whatever price we agreed upon). Of course, by doing so I would then have forgone the receipt of future interest. As the new creditor, he would instead have been entitled to it. But I would have also made a $1,000 profit over and above what I earned while owning the loan. While selling the loan agreement was another avenue I could have

NOTES

used to profit, it was also an exit strategy I could have employed if I needed to recuperate my money.

I should point out that executing on Section 8 isn't as simple as putting a loan agreement up on Craigslist. You will have to find a qualified buyer. As well, depending on where you live, there might be regulations that govern how and to whom such a sale is made.

NOTES

SECTION 5

# DUE DILIGENCE

Adequately researching an investment is of the utmost importance to its success and security. As an investor, I strive to understand every element of risk – business, market and otherwise – before deploying my capital into a project.

Unlike the stock market, measures like *dividend yield* and *earnings per share* are of little meaning in private deals done with entrepreneurs. There are no ticker symbols or 52-week price graphs that one can search for on Google Finance. Moreover, small businesses are not required to produce audited financial statements, issue reports to shareholders or make any information available to the public. They are *private* businesses, which, so long as they pay their taxes and obey regulations, are not required to disclose anything to anyone.

NOTES

The opacity of a small business can pose difficulties to a person seeking to make an investment into one. How reliable is your due diligence if you can't verify the accuracy of your research? This is one of the greatest risks involved with investing with an entrepreneur.

As such, probing a private business will usually require a combination of aggressive investigating, knowing what questions to ask, understanding the legal ramifications of the deal and confirming the validity of your findings. It will also require a certain degree of trust built through relationships and common sense, which I will address later on in this section.

The bulk of my due diligence on BIR was done over the phone and through email, which you can view in Exhibit A. Below is a short list of some of the main risks that I faced when making this investment.

NOTES

## Some potential risks of investing into BIR

- **Failure and collapse of BIR**

Since this investment was assembled as a loan and not as a purchase of shares in the company, the ultimate success of BIR was not paramount to me. I did not need it to become an ultra-profitable venture. Instead, the business simply had to be able to produce enough revenue to service its payments and return my capital within two years.

BIR's failure, however, would have added an enormous amount of risk to the deal. Since it operated an ice skating rink, it did not own easily-saleable assets like real estate. It would therefore have been challenging to recoup my capital from it. In the event of BIR's demise, I would have likely been forced to rely on Laura, personally, to repay me.

NOTES

• **Laura entering into personal bankruptcy**

Bankruptcy is a term that is often used loosely and incorrectly. To "go bankrupt" is not to own a failed business or to be very poor. Instead, one goes bankrupt when they are functionally unable to repay their debts. It is a legal status that is declared by the court.

Technically speaking, BIR, not Laura, was in debt to me. However, if the company was unable to repay the loan I could have then enforced the letter of guarantee and compelled her to do so. At that point she would have become my debtor.

If Laura applied for personal bankruptcy and received approval, the court may have forced her to repay some of the money she owed through a sale of her remaining assets, such as her home. It could also have allowed her creditors to garnish some of her future earnings. However, it is likely that she would have been absolved of most or all of her debts, including of the guarantee to me. In such a case, I would have lost my investment altogether. To that end, the potential for Laura to go bankrupt was the greatest risk involved in this deal.

NOTES

• **Lack of liquidity on the loan**

The loan to BIR was a highly **illiquid** (hard to sell) investment. Unless the company repaid me in advance or I sold the loan agreement to someone else, there was little chance that I could have recouped the $25,000 before two years. As such, if there was an emergency during that time or if I had an immediate need for money, the investment would not have been of much use to me. Unlike buying blue-chip stocks through an online brokerage, I could not have simply pushed a button to sell my investment into BIR.

Each person has her own liquidity preferences. Some people desire a portfolio that can be converted into cash almost instantly. Others are willing to accept less saleability. I, personally, value cash immensely. Not only can it get you out of a bind, but having cash on hand allows you to take advantage of good buying opportunities. For example, if the price of a stock was to fall to a steep discount, only investors with funds available could capitalize on such a deal.

Since much of my portfolio is locked into private investments, I produce my cash by purchasing

NOTES

assets that pay a monthly income. Although I may not be able to sell most of my holdings within minutes, I always have funds available thanks to the revenue they generate.

- **Changes in market interest rates**

Interest rates in the market change constantly. In well-managed economies the change is usually gradual, but it can prove substantial over time. For instance, in the United States, the interest earned on savings kept with a bank in the 1980s often hovered between 7% and 14%. Between 2008 and 2015, however, those same accounts usually paid less than half of one percent in interest.

The risk of interest rate changes can materially impact the competitiveness of an investment like the one that I made into BIR. For example, if I could have earned 12% by placing my capital into a savings account, this deal would have been far less attractive. Why go through the efforts of performing due diligence, creating loan agreements and personal guarantees and potentially going to court when I could simply lump my cash into a bank for the same return?

NOTES

Although rising interest may not have damaged my investment into BIR, they could have made it much less lucrative when compared to other deals. As such, the risk would not necessarily have been in a capital loss (unless it was an exorbitant increase), but rather in the opportunity cost.

**LEARNING POINT** Risk does not always entail losing money. It can also mean missing out on other opportunities.

Furthermore, interest rate increases are often associated with **inflation** control. Inflation, which is the rising costs of goods and services in an economy, essentially means that the value of currency declines over time. In Canada and the US, that usually means that our money is worth about 3% less each year. Buying a pair of jeans for $100 in 2016, for instance, might cost $103 in 2017.

Investors, then, should deduct the cost of inflation from their return on investment to calculate their real **rate of return**. In the case of BIR, since annual inflation in Canada was 2% and I made 12% on the

NOTES

deal, my actual rate of return was only 10% per year. Not only does inflation threaten the merits of the investment altogether (for example, if inflation was 15% I would have lost money), but it can cause the government to raise interest rates to counteract its effects.

- **Key person risk**

BIR was mostly managed by Laura and Dave. Unlike a multibillion dollar corporation with thousands of employees, small businesses often are deeply impacted by individual members of staff. If something happened to either of them, BIR would have likely collapsed. Laura's death or incapacitation would have therefore materially threatened my ability to recoup the investment, since she not only owned the company but also personally guaranteed the loan to it.

NOTES

## Information that I required from Dave and Laura about BIR

To manage some of the aforementioned risks, I asked Dave a series of questions to which I required answers in writing. I've included explanations for those questions below as well as why I felt them to be pertinent to ask.

- **What is the name and registered address of the entity I'm lending to?**

To complete the Loan Agreement, I needed to know the legal name of Laura's company, which was BC Ice Rinks Ltd. (the suffix, "Ltd.," stands for "limited liability," referencing the fact that it is a separate legal entity from its owners, who are therefore not liable for its debt). BC Ice Rinks Ltd. would then be the corporation that would contractually borrow funds from my company. It is also referred to in the letter of guarantee.

Note that some firms have **"DBAs"** (Doing Business As) or **"trade names,"** which are the names under which they advertise and do business. Those titles are different from their legal names. For instance, I once had a numbered company (eg. 1234567 BC

NOTES

Ltd.) that was referred to as Assadi Capital. While I may have promoted it as Assadi Capital, any contracts that it entered into were done through 1234567 BC Ltd.

Addresses are often included in contracts for identification purposes. For instance, rather than "John Smith" signing an agreement, a contract would typically identify him as "John Smith, an individual with a residence at 123 Gingerbread Road, Toronto, Ontario, Canada."

In my opinion, it is less important to include a corporation's address in a contract than it is for a person. While there may be 10,000 John Smiths, in Canada no two corporations can have a same or even a very similar name, so it is easy to identify which company entered into the agreement. Moreover, corporations are required to update the **corporate registry** with their office address. So if I needed to communicate with BIR in writing or file a lawsuit against it, I could have simply found its address by doing a corporate search. Regardless, I still requested BIR's registered and records address.

NOTES

**LEARNING POINT** Corporations often have suffixes like, Ltd., Inc., LLC., Corporation, Corp., Pty. Ltd. and GmbH. You should be acquainted with these.

- **Is BIR the same entity that currently owns your wife's ice rink business and will it own it in the future?**

It might appear self-evident that BC Ice Rinks Ltd. would operate an ice rink, but that may not, in fact, have been the case. Remember that businesses often use the corporate veil to protect their assets. It is common for one corporation to manage the operations of a company while another one owns the physical assets. As such, if the operating company is sued or files for bankruptcy, it may not have a material impact on the general business.

Larger organizations will often even create a separate **shell corporation** (a corporation with no real assets) solely for payroll purposes. If a company was successfully sued by a former employee, it then could be argued that the employer was the shell and it might therefore incur little financial harm.

NOTES ______

I have even seen firms concoct shell corporations for the sole purpose of borrowing money. Once the shell receives the loan, it then lends it out to related corporations for them to use. However, those companies would be protected from the liabilities of the shell corporation.

With the above in mind, since I did not know how Dave and Laura organized their business, I wanted them to represent to me in writing that BIR owned and operated the ice rink. If it was later discovered that the company did not, I could potentially have sued them for making a fraudulent misrepresentation.

**LEARNING POINT** Shell corporations are typically employed to protect a person's or a company's assets. They are used frequently by both small businesses and large conglomerates. Be sure that you know whether your borrower is a shell

NOTES

**• Is BIR profitable?**

It is far riskier to lend to a money-losing business than to one that is profitable. A profitable company is more likely to have the resources to repay you.

**• Does BIR have any debt? Does it plan on taking on more debt, except for the purpose of refinancing my loan?**

It was important for me to know whether BIR owed money to anyone else. I did not want to be just one out of a long line of creditors. As you can see from Dave's response, the firm actually did carry some debt. However, I happened to know that lender personally and I was familiar with the particulars of the loan. Aside from him, though, nobody else had loaned funds to BIR.

Understanding a business' debt situation can be fairly complex. In general, not only do I want to know the interest rates, terms and conditions with the other lenders, but I also want to know my priority. That is, in the event of a default, who gets paid out first and what specific claims do the creditors have on the company's assets? As a lender, I want

NOTES

to have the first or at least the second position on them. Laura's personal guarantee, however, made this information less important to me, especially since I knew that she had assets (other businesses and real estate) outside of the ice rink business.

Note the last part of my question: "Except for the purpose of refinancing my loan." When the term of the loan matured, BIR might have chosen to borrow money from someone else in order to pay me out. That is known as **refinancing**, which I obviously had no qualms with. I did not mind how BIR repaid me, just so long as it was done.

- **Describe specifically what the loan will be used for**

In my opinion, a company that needs funds to grow is probably healthier than one that needs money to pay down its debts. If BIR sought a loan to pay its credit cards instead of to buy revenue-producing assets, the deal may not have been as attractive to me. Knowing this information was important not only for me to understand my risk, but also to satisfy my personal preferences as an investor. I enjoy helping businesses expand rather than refinancing their loans.

NOTES

**• If Laura was to die or become incapacitated, what would happen to the ice rink?**

This question was asked in order to address the key person risk. I wanted to know whether a contingency plan was in place in the case of Laura's death or inability to work. What would have happened to BIR if she could no longer run it? Some companies, for example, have succession plans where other staff would automatically replace the deceased manager. Most small businesses, though, cannot easily do that. As such, losing a company's key person can yield disastrous results for investors.

Dave responded to my question by advising that Laura had a life insurance policy worth $750,000. Those funds could be available if I had to recoup my loan from her estate. Such policies usually don't cover suicide, though.

NOTES

- **The Loan Agreement will contain a General Security Agreement, which will give me first claim on all the assets the ice rink owns. Do you have an issue with this?**

In the event of a default, a **General Security Agreement** (GSA) would have provided me with a claim on all of BIR's assets. It would have helped mitigate my risk, since the company already had some debt and could potentially incur more in the future. Although GSAs can look strong on paper, they are often impractical when dealing with businesses that don't have liquid assets. If I was to enforce a GSA, would I really seize BIR's vending machines, cash registers, ice skates and food inventory and try to sell them?

As you can tell from our email exchanges, Dave was also uncomfortable with a GSA and preferred that the loan was primarily secured by the equipment for which it was used to buy. In Exhibit B, you can see that I asked my lawyer to draft a GSA. But I eventually decided that it would not add security to my investment and I chose not to include it in the deal.

NOTES

## Trust, common sense and relationships

Compared to other investments I have made, the research that I did on the BIR deal was relatively minimal. Although Dave and I spoke on the phone several times and sent emails back and forth, I never even once corresponded with Laura. The only "communication" we had was that both of our signatures were on the same piece of paper when we executed the loan agreement. So why was I comfortable enough to do this deal when my due diligence was so light?

As I have mentioned earlier, Dave and I had known each other for years and had done business together before. Prior to his reaching out to me on behalf of his wife, I already had a good understanding of their financial position and their expanding business empire. In addition to knowing about their real estate and commercial achievements, we also had mutual associates that could verify the success of their own investments with Dave. And most importantly, Dave and Laura had a track record of making me money.

NOTES

There was also a degree of trust and partnership that we had extended to one another over the years. In exchange for issuing credit to him almost upon request, Dave offered me early access to his best investment opportunities. I almost looked at our relationship as comparable to a bank's with a long-term client. The bank will offer its client a healthy line of credit at a reasonable interest rate, so long as the client makes timely payments and fulfills his contractual obligations. Similar to a bank, there was also a maximum amount of credit that I would have extended to Dave. But as long as I kept earning profits with him and I did not feel like too much of my portfolio was invested with him, I was comfortable with continuing our relationship.

There are some investments that I will approach like a police detective. I will request financial statements, I will ask for taxation history, business plans, proof of sales, proof of orders, inventory valuations, etc. I will also place a lien on the entrepreneur's properties, vehicles and other assets of value. Dave

NOTES

and Laura did not fall into that boat, not because I trusted them blindly, but because I considered my due diligence on them having spanned several years. If it was my first time doing business with them, I would not have been as lax.

Of course, my trust in Dave and Laura only extended so far. As you have already seen, I did not afford them the protection of a corporation. Even though I was certain that they would do anything to pay me back – I was not certain enough to release them of a personal encumbrance.

With that said, not every partner is deserving of the same amount of trust. A bond is built over time. If you are at the very beginning of a relationship or are making a new type of investment, your due diligence should be thorough. If this was my first time working with Dave, my approach would have been much different. Below are the requirements I would have demanded from BIR and Laura prior to making the investment.

NOTES ______________________________

## Administrative

- **BIR and Laura must sign an engagement letter**

Performing due diligence can cost money. It might require hiring lawyers and consultants, pulling title searches on properties and discovering credit scores, etc. But what would happen if I spent funds on the research and decided not to move forward with the investment into BIR? I would have potentially wasted thousands of dollars.

To mitigate such an occurrence, I would have presented BIR and Laura with a **letter of engagement**. This document would inform them that I was interested in doing business together, but that my investment would be contingent on their satisfaction of the due diligence requirements therein stipulated. It would also state that all costs that I incurred while doing research must be reimbursed, regardless of whether the deal closed.

- **Request copies of BIR's articles of incorporation**

**Articles of incorporation** are the documents used to form a corporation. They include important details, like its legal and share structure, registered

NOTES

and records address as well as who the officers and directors of the firm are. I would have requested copies of the articles of incorporation for BC Ice Rinks Ltd. to confirm that the company actually existed and that it was created in accordance with the applicable laws.

**LEARNING POINT** A corporation is controlled by its shareholders. The shareholders appoint the corporation's directors, who are, in turn, responsible to manage the company.

- **Request proof of BIR's good standing with the corporate registry**

Corporations must remain in good standing with the provincial/federal/state corporate registries. This is typically as simple as filing financial reports and paying annual fees. Failure to do so, however, can result in the company being struck from the registry and dissolved. As such, I would have requested proof of BIR's good standing to confirm that the corporation wasn't at risk of administrative dissolution.

NOTES

**• Request proof of signing authority of the officers and/or directors of BIR**

Only certain people, usually directors and officers, have the authority to bind a corporation into a contract. Since BIR was going to sign an agreement with my investment company, I would have requested proof that its representative (Laura) had the ability to do so on behalf of the firm. If she didn't, it could have been argued that our agreement was invalid.

There are two documents that I might have required for proof: First, a notarized sworn **affidavit** (a statement sworn under oath) from Laura to that effect. Second, a resolution from the directors (a **Directors' Resolutio**n, see Exhibit E for an example) of BIR delegating signing authority to her. Moreover, I would have included the following phrase under Laura's signature line in the loan agreement: "I have the authority to bind this corporation into this Agreement."

NOTES

**LEARNING POINT** A Directors' Resolution is a formal action that has been voted on by the corporation's directors. It is often required for any important corporate decision to be made.

- **Request that Laura does not sign the loan agreement on behalf of BIR**

If BIR had other directors aside from Laura (this could be discovered in the articles of incorporation), I would have requested that one of them, instead of she, signed the loan agreement on behalf of the company. Laura would have only executed the letter of guarantee. This would add further separation between all parties involved. It would have made it more difficult for both BIR and Laura to argue that they were unknowingly or unfairly bound by contracts that they did not want to sign.

NOTES

**• Request a resolution of the directors of BIR to authorize the loan**

Regardless of whether Laura was the sole director of BIR, I would have required proof that the company's managers had formally authorized it to borrow money from me and that nobody was acting beyond their capacities. As with the above paragraph, this would help ensure that claims of ignorance about the loan could not be made. Thus, I would have requested a directors' resolution to that effect.

**• Request certificates of independent legal advice for BIR and Laura**

To add even greater distinction between BIR and Laura, I would have requested that each party be represented in the deal by a different attorney. Both lawyers would write letters to me confirming that they had provided independent legal advice to their client. That would have made it harder to argue that either party received conflicting counsel. Otherwise, for example, BIR might have claimed that its lawyer advised it with Laura's interests, not the company's, in mind.

NOTES

**LEARNING POINT** Each party should be represented by its own lawyer. Conflicts of interest can muddle agreements and, in some cases, ruin an investment.

**• Request an affidavit from BIR confirming that it is the owner and operator of the ice rink and stating that it has no intention to go bankrupt**

To ensure that BIR was indeed the entity that owned Dave and Laura's ice rink and that it did not plan on filing for bankruptcy, I would have required a sworn affidavit to that effect.

## Financial

**• Request net worth statements from both BIR and Laura outlining all of their assets and liabilities**

A **net worth statement** (Exhibit F) would help paint a picture of BIR and Laura's financial positions. It would have described what they owned and what they owed (including loans that they guaranteed or co-signed for). If BIR had a lot of debt, then that would have

NOTES

likely hampered its ability to service my loan. If Laura was deeply indebted, that may have encumbered my ability to collect from her if BIR defaulted on its obligations. A net worth statement would have ultimately helped me better assess my risk.

After viewing the statement, if I had discovered that BIR and Laura had substantial amounts of debt, I may have then requested further information about the details of the loans. What specific claims on assets did their creditors have? When did they mature? What interest rates did they carry? That knowledge would have helped me understand whether my loan could reasonably be repaid.

- **Request proof that BIR and Laura are current with their tax obligations**

In most cases, the government has first claim on both a person's and on a company's assets if they do not pay their taxes. For example, if you own a piece of real estate but have not paid your income tax, the government could seize your property and sell it in order to recoup your liabilities. This is regardless if other creditors have claims on that property too.

NOTES

To manage the risk of the government appropriating their assets before I was repaid, I would have requested proof that both BIR and Laura were current on all tax obligations. I would have required copies of their **tax returns** for the previous two years, as well as a sworn affidavit from their accountants to confirm their good standing.

**LEARNING POINT** If a person owes taxes, the government can seize their assets, including real estate, vehicles and shares in companies. The government has priority over ther creditors in this regard.

• **Request proof of both BIR and Laura's incomes for the previous two years**

Most lenders will only provide funds to borrowers if they meet a certain debt-to-income ratio. If a borrower's income is barely high enough to service his debt obligations, he is viewed as a high-risk client. As such, it is important to know how much the borrower earns.

NOTES

The aforementioned tax returns would have shed light on BIR and Laura's incomes. However, in addition, I would have requested **financial statements** for BIR that had been audited by an independent accountant. Internally-produced statements can be easily altered to skew the numbers in favour of the borrower.

- **Perform credit checks on BIR and Laura**

To better understand their histories of paying bills and repaying debts, I would have sought authorization to pull credit reports on both BIR and Laura. Some jurisdictions have strict laws about performing credit checks on others, so if I could not have done so with relative ease, I would have then requested that BIR and Laura conducted checks on themselves and then advanced the results to me.

- **Request a business plan along with two-year projections**

Although the above information would provide me with an understanding of BIR and Laura's past, I would also have required projections about the company's future earnings to help assess its ability to service the loan. To do so, I would request a

NOTES

detailed business plan that explained the vending machines' revenue model as well as income and profit predictions for the business as a whole.

**LEARNING POINT** Not all debts appear on a credit bureau. Don't rely solely on a credit report to find out what people owe,

## Practical

- **Request insurance**

Since this investment into BIR was subjected to key person risk, I would have required Laura to assign her life insurance policy to my investment company. As such, if she died I would have then received the proceeds up until my loan was repaid.

For additional security, another option would have been to request that BIR purchases a "key person" insurance policy, which would provide a payout to the company in the event of Laura's death or incapacitation. Key person insurance, however, is often expensive and might be unfeasible for a small business to acquire.

NOTES

• **Include a floating interest rate on the loan**

To mitigate the risk of erosion due to inflation or interest rate changes, I could have structured the interest rate on the loan as a **floating rate.** Thus, rather than charging a fixed 12%, I would have chosen a widely-recognized benchmark rate and added interest to that.

For example, since this was a Canadian loan, I would have chosen the **Bank of Canada's Overnight Rate** (0.5% at the time of writing) plus an additional 11.5%. If the Overnight Rate increased, which would signal a pending overall interest rate hike, the interest on my loan would swell automatically.

**LEARNING POINT** A floating interest rate "floats" with the benchmark.

• **Place a mortgage on Laura and/or BIR's real estate**

From their net worth statements, I would have been able to determine whether Laura and BIR owned any real estate. Unlike most other collateral, a property is usually relatively simple to foreclose upon. As security for my loan, I could have then

NOTES

requested that a **mortgage** was placed on some or all of their real estate holdings until it was repaid. If a default occurred, I could have then seized and sold those assets in order to recoup my capital. If there was already a mortgage on their properties, I could have placed a second (or third) mortgage on them. This is also relatively simple to do with automobiles.

I should note that using a lawyer for this is not only recommended, but it is often required. A mortgage is typically registered with the government; where I live, it is the Land Title and Survey Authority of BC, which may only accept submissions from licensed attorneys.

Moreover, some lenders will prohibit subsequent mortgages from being placed behind theirs. For example, if a bank has a mortgage on a property, it may not allow the owner to accept additional mortgages on it. If another debt is placed on the real estate and the bank discovers it, it may trigger a **default event** (an event that is considered a default under the loan agreement). A lawyer can help you determine whether mortgaging a property is a feasible or a good idea.

NOTES

**LEARNING POINT** If there is a pre-existing mortgage on a property, review the loan agreement made between the borrower and the first lender to verify whether a second mortgage can be placed on it.

- **Include a "default events" clause**

The loan agreement signed between BIR and my investment company permitted me to demand immediate repayment of the loan if the borrower defaulted on its obligations. For further protection, however, I could have broadened the scope of what a "default" was to include BIR and/or Laura's failure to pay taxes, failure to make the appropriate administrative filings, the acceptance of additional debt and any material detrimental changes to their financial positions.

Essentially, if my risk increased throughout the term of the loan, this clause would permit me to recall it without BIR necessarily missing any payments.

NOTES

**• Include the ability to demand repayment at any time**

For additional security, the loan agreement could have stated that the loan can be recalled at any time, for any reason and without explanation to the borrower. While this could place BIR under substantial financial pressure if enforced, it would also help address my liquidity risk. If I needed my $25,000 back quickly, such a clause would have allowed me to request an immediate repayment of it.

**• Increase the monthly payment amount**

The loan agreement stipulated that BIR would make a minimum monthly payment of $250, which would first be applied against its interest obligations and then to any fees outstanding. In two years, it would make a $25,000 principal payment. To accelerate the rate at which I retrieved my capital, I could have requested a larger monthly payment, which would also regularly eat into the principal sum. For instance, if the monthly payment was $1,176.84, then BIR would have repaid the loan in 24 equal instalments and would not need to make a large deposit upon the loan's maturity.

NOTES

While this strategy can help the lender recoup the loan faster, an unreasonably high monthly payment can put pressure on the borrower. If too many of the borrower's resources are required to meet those payments, it could threaten its business and therefore the security of the loan. As such, one should take care to find a balance. In some cases, when cash flow is a concern, a lender will only require one whole payment of interest and principal upon maturity, rather than on a monthly schedule.

NOTES

SECTION 6

# CONCLUSION

My investment into BIR was ultimately a balancing act. It meant respecting my friendship and partnership with Dave, while at the same time asking tough, personal questions and compelling his wife to sign an agreement that could prove devastating if she broke it. I needed to find an equilibrium that not only satisfied business with pleasure, but one that also recognized that damaging our partnership could cost me a fortune in the future.

In my mind, one of the greatest risks of this deal was in opportunity cost: if I demanded too much from Dave and Laura - if I exercised all of my due diligence options - would they have been offended and cancelled the loan? Would they have approached another lender and even excluded

NOTES

me from subsequent investments? After all, I am not their only business partner and I am not the first person to have done well with them. At the same time, I have worked hard for my assets and I deserve the ability to protect them. Where does one draw the line?

Relationship management is one of the most under-discussed features of investments into private companies. I could write a thousand case studies with asset protection strategies, but they would be of little value without a good bond with a great entrepreneur.

An outsider might perhaps say, "Well, business is business. If Dave and Laura want you to invest, they should then set aside their egos, feelings and pride and answer any question that you present them with." But in my opinion, using blanket statements like "business is business" is unfair and amateurish.

First, unlike buying or selling stocks, deals like BIR are done through *people* – all of whom obviously have feelings. In this case, I was not negotiating with salaried officers of a multibillion dollar corporation. I was dealing with two small business owners who

NOTES

built their flourishing company up from nothing. Demanding that someone pretends that emotions don't exist, or temporarily discards them, is not always feasible.

Second, Dave, Laura and I were negotiating from a level playing field. Neither party necessarily had any leverage over the other. BIR was not desperate for a loan. My $25,000 was not going to be used to bail out the company and save it from impending insolvency. Instead, it was to buy a few vending machines. If I pushed too hard, Dave and Laura could have simply said, "Listen, we're giving you an easy way to make money here. We've done nothing for you in the past *except* to make you money. We're going to take this deal to another one of our investors who trusts what we do." It would be as simple as sending a text message. Unlike buying stocks, which is largely a function of mathematical calculation, relationships must be respected in this realm of business.

Nonetheless, it still is crucial to ensure that your capital is secure. A large loss can wipe out years of returns and can greatly set you back. As I stressed

NOTES

in my book, Rich At 26, my experience is that private investments with entrepreneurs can yield phenomenal returns – *if* the correct steps are taken to mitigate risk.

Now, when it comes to traditional investing, risk management is often as simple as hedging with options (puts, calls, etc.). Although my intent is not to minimize the skill involved with trading stocks, it is fair to say that there are often more moving pieces when placing funds with small business owners: performing credit checks, hiring lawyers, etc. If you look at my due diligence list in this case study, none of those requirement s can be searched for on Google Finance. There were no analysts that I could have subscribed to who give opinions on BIR. And I couldn't have made the investment by simply clicking a button online.

Ironically, a lot of active effort is required for a passive income deal like this one to work. It cost me several thousand dollars just to learn the basic legal topics I discussed in this case study. I have spent hours learning from experts in the field and lost money on failed opportunities. But after years of practice, investments like these are now second

NOTES

nature to me. I rarely consider traditional assets anymore because of how lucrative deals like BIR can be.

While this case study documented the steps that I took to make an investment with an entrepreneur, it should be recognized that it was only a snapshot in time. It detailed the acquisition of single asset, but it doesn't characterize my portfolio as a whole. Each transaction is different and varies based on my due diligence requirements, relationship with the business owner and assessment of the risk involved. There is, and can be, no template to investing with entrepreneurs. The range of businesses is too broad, the people are too diverse and the laws are too different.

Instead, I believe that one becomes savvy in these types of opportunities through calculated trial and error. My experience began with simplistic deals and I gradually moved on to more complicated ones. Over time, I made connections with other investors, small business owners, lawyers and professionals from whom I could learn. With each investment came new obstacles and thus new ways to gain experience. In fact, you can see my progression in

NOTES

my investment agreements, which started out as half-page contracts and advanced towards what they are today.

My current investments are culminations of years of experimentation, networking and a commitment to improving my craft. At the time of writing I have completed upwards of 70 similar deals. That track record has engrained not only some measure of technical expertise, but also common sense and "gut feeling" intelligence that a less seasoned investor may not yet possess.

For instance, people who are new to the world of entrepreneurship commonly forget about the flexibility of our industry. They will often make an investment using contracts that are drawn up by the small business owner and that are more favorable to the receiving entity. However, an invaluable lesson that I've learned is that if you have capital to invest, then *you* should be in the driver's seat. The terms and conditions of the deal should largely be dictated by the person with money, not by the one asking for it. When I ask a new investor why they didn't make alterations to the agreement that they signed, their response is often, "I didn't know I could do that."

NOTES

While it may seem obvious here, that is something that is *learned*; it isn't innate information.

Know-how aside, an investor's gut feeling can be her most valuable asset. In early 2015 I considered purchasing real estate in a small town in central Alberta, only minutes away from a large oil excavation project. The entrepreneur with whom I intended to work was well-known as a skilled property manager who could perform low-cost, quality renovations. After noticing discrepancies between what he said and what was put into writing, however, I became uncomfortable and cancelled the deal altogether. I later discovered that the town's real estate prices fell by 50% after the oil company departed, and I thus avoided a disaster. I'm fairly certain that a "younger me," though, would have trusted the entrepreneur because of his reputation and ignored the warning signs.

With the emphasis on experience in mind, if you would like to explore doing a deal like the one I did with Dave and Laura, I would caution you to tread carefully. Remember that a key challenge with these investments is the opacity of small businesses. Performing adequate due diligence is imperative

NOTES

to your success. As you explore an investment opportunity, jot down every pitfall – big or small – and every way you might lose money that you can think of. Bring the deal to people you know and ask them to try to poke holes in it. You could even search online. Think of *anything* that could cause the project to fail: a lack of demand from customers, death, earthquakes, cost overruns, etc. – no situation is too ridiculous. Identifying every possible risk should comprise the beginning of your research.

Once each problem has been pinpointed, then try to match it with a solution. For instance, you will recall that I identified BIR's corporate veil as a risk, so I circumvented it by having Laura sign a personal guarantee. Your solutions should ultimately shape the structure of the investment. It should then further be refined to maximize profits. For example, if you think that the contemplated business has enormous growth potential, then you may not want to make a debt investment into it. Instead, you might seek to capitalize on its growth by purchasing equity or structuring it so that the debt

NOTES

could later convert to shares. On the other hand, if you believe that there is too much risk involved or simply prefer the income that a loan can provide, you might opt to structure it similarly to my deal with BIR. Malleability is the beauty of investing with entrepreneurs.

Perhaps you're in the market for your first private investment. Maybe you know a person who flips houses. You might have a friend who is launching a smartphone app. Maybe there are local entrepreneurship events that you could attend to broaden your network. You never know where the next home run is hiding. Investing in companies like BIR can be a complex exercise and one that certainly can't be learned overnight. But when done correctly, participating in deals like these can be a most rewarding experience.

NOTES

EXHIBIT A

# EMAIL EXCHANGES WITH DAVE

**Alexis Assadi <                @gmail.com>**

# Deal

13 messages

**Alexis Assadi** <                @gmail.com> Sat, Aug 22, 2015 at 9:31 AM
To: **Dave** <dave@                .com>

I'm up island with bad reception so not sure if you got my text last night. I'm in for $25k. Let's discuss more next week.

Alexis Assadi

Sent from my iPhone

**Dave** <dave@                .com> Sat, Aug 22, 2015 at 9:32 AM
To: **Alexis Assadi** <                @gmail.com>

Sounds good brother.  I'll start the process on my end and call you Monday.

[Quoted text hidden]

**Alexis Assadi** <                @gmail.com> Sat, Aug 22, 2015 at 10:04 AM
To: **Dave** <dave@                .com>

I'd like to use one of my contracts. That cool?

Alexis Assadi
Assadi Global Ventures, Inc.

Sent from my iPhone

[Quoted text hidden]

**Dave** <dave@                .com> Sat, Aug 22, 2015 at 11:02 AM
To: **Alexis Assadi** <                @gmail.com>

Yes i will pass it off to Jon after I receive it.

Can we meet the time lines I spoke about.

[Quoted text hidden]

**Alexis Assadi** < @gmail.com> Sat, Aug 22, 2015 at 11:11 AM
To: **Dave** <dave@ .com>

Yes. I'll have a contract ready for Monday. I'll mail the cheque as soon as its signed. That work?

Alexis Assadi
Assadi Global Ventures, Inc.

Sent from my iPhone

[Quoted text hidden]

---

**Dave** <dave@ .com> Sat, Aug 22, 2015 at 11:12 AM
To: **Alexis Assadi** < @gmail.com>

Yes. Thanks bud!

[Quoted text hidden]

---

**Alexis Assadi** < @gmail.com> Sat, Aug 22, 2015 at 12:20 PM
To: **Dave** <dave@ .com>

No problem. Can you please send me the following:

1. Name of the entity I'm lending to.
2. Registered address of the entity I'm lending to
3. Name and registered address of the guarantor

Alexis Assadi
Assadi Global Ventures, Inc.

Sent from my iPhone

[Quoted text hidden]

---

**Dave** <dave@ .com> Sat, Aug 22, 2015 at 3:26 PM
To: **Alexis Assadi** < @gmail.com>

1. Ltd.
2. # - BC .
3. Same address for gauranteur.

[Quoted text hidden]

**Alexis Assadi** < @gmail.com> Sat, Aug 22, 2015 at 4:44 PM
To: **Dave** <dave@ .com>

Thanks. A few questions:

1. Is that entity the same one that currently owns your wife's ice rink business and will own it in the future?
2. Is her ice rink profitable?
3. Does her ice rink have any debt?
4. Describe specifically what the loan will be used for
5. Does her ice rink business plan to take on more debt, except for the purpose of refinancing my loan?
6. Sorry. I have to ask this one! If your wife was to die or become incapacitated, what would happen to the ice rink?
7. The loan agreement will contain a general security agreement, which gives me first claim on all assets the ice rink owns. Do you have an issue with this?

Alexis Assadi
Assadi Global Ventures, Inc.

Sent from my iPhone

[Quoted text hidden]

**Dave** <dave@ .com> Sat, Aug 22, 2015 at 7:42 PM
To: **Alexis Assadi** < @gmail.com>

1. yes
2. The ice rink currently profits $5,000 per month.
3. The ice rink has $20,000 in total debt( ). This is the only loan has ever taken to grow her business:)
4. The loan will be specifically for a . (I emailed you the and specifics.)
5. If the goes as well as planned a second will be purchased after the first is paid for. The current office move and expansion adding 4 additional vending machines is all being done with retained earnings of the Corp.
6. If passes the ice rink will be sold. To that end $750,000 in life insurance on is in place.
7. I would prefer the security agreement places claim on the as far as assets go. And the remainder of the recovery on cash flow in such a situation.

Thoughts?

[Quoted text hidden]

**Alexis Assadi** < @gmail.com> Sat, Aug 22, 2015 at 8:06 PM
To: **Dave** <dave@ .com>

Ok cool. Let's chat more on Monday about security. Need to be able to get my $$ out if shit hits the fan lol.

Alexis Assadi
Assadi Global Ventures, Inc.

Sent from my iPhone

[Quoted text hidden]

---

**Dave** <dave@ .com> Sat, Aug 22, 2015 at 8:23 PM
To: **Alexis Assadi** < @gmail.com>

Roger that! Have a great weekend!

[Quoted text hidden]

---

**Alexis Assadi** < @gmail.com> Sat, Aug 22, 2015 at 8:27 PM
To: **Dave** <dave@ .com>

You too!

Alexis Assadi
Assadi Global Ventures, Inc.

Sent from my iPhone

[Quoted text hidden]

**Alexis Assadi <** 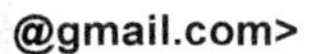 **@gmail.com>**

---

## Loan Agreement/Letter of Guarantee

2 messages

**Alexis Assadi** < @gmail.com> Wed, Aug 26, 2015 at 5:34 PM
To: **Dave** <dave@ .com>

Hey,

Attached are two documents: a loan agreement and a letter of guarantee. If you and your wife are good with everything in there, please ask your wife to sign these and email them back to me. Once I've received them, I'll sign and send over the cash.

Just a heads-up: there are a few spots that your wife will need to initial within the contracts.

For my convenience, can you please mail the documents to the office in (note that this address is different than the one in the agreement)? The address is

Talk to you soon,

Alexis Assadi
www.AlexisAssadi.com
Assadi Global Ventures, Inc.

**2 attachments**

PDF Adobe **Loan Agreement Unsigned.pdf**
166K

**Personal Guarantee Unsigned.pdf**
91K

**Dave** <dave@ .com> Wed, Aug 26, 2015 at 5:46 PM
To: **Alexis Assadi** < @gmail.com>

She will review them tonight with me:)

Have a great evening!

PS. When are you sending me a hard copy of your book?

[Quoted text hidden]

--

Phone:
Email:
Address:

IMPORTANT: The contents of this email and any attachments are confidential. They are intended for the named recipient(s) only. If you have received this email by mistake, please notify the sender immediately and do not disclose the contents to anyone or make copies thereof.

**Alexis Assadi < @gmail.com>**

---

## Cheque

1 messages

---

**Alexis Assadi** < @gmail.com> Thu, Aug 27, 2015 at 12:57 PM
To: **Dave** <dave@ .com>

Hey,

I just mailed a package to you. It's got my book, and inside the book is the cheque for $25k.

Chat soon

Alexis Assadi
Assadi Global Ventures, Inc.

Sent from my iPhone

Alexis

EXHIBIT B

# EMAIL EXCHANGES WITH MY LAWYER

On Aug 22, 2015, at 11:24 AM, Alexis Assadi <aassadi@ .com> wrote:

I'm lending $25k to 's wife. She has a ice rink and is . Do you have a general security agreement you could send? It's not urgent. The deal will take place in 10 days.

Also, are you able to talk on the phone today for 10 min?

-

Alexis S. Assadi
**Supreme Overlord,**
**Assadi Global Ventures, Inc.**
*Investing in Entrepreneurs.*

---

**From**: < @ .com>
**Date**: August 22, 2015 at 10:33:20 AM PDT
**To**: Alexis Assadi <aassadi@ .com>
**Subject: Re: New deal**

I will do up a GSA during the week and send it to you. The one we did for would likely work. I just want to check up on any difference between BC laws that would require changes.

Sure. Call me between 2 and 4.

Sent from my iPhone

EXHIBIT C

---

# LOAN AGREEMENT

THIS LOAN AGREEMENT ("**Agreement**") made the th day of August 2015 ("**Effective Date**").

BETWEEN:

**ASSADI ,**

a corporation incorporated under the laws of the Province of British Columbia and having its registered and records office at - Avenue, , British Columbia, (the "**Lender**")

- and –

**LTD.,**

a corporation incorporated under the laws of British Columbia and having its registered and records office at # - Street, , British Columbia,

(the "**Borrower**")

**IN CONSIDERATION** of the premises and covenants and agreements hereinafter contained it is agreed by and between the parties as follows:

**Section 1: Loan Amount**

On September 2nd 2015, the Lender will loan to the Borrower $25,000 in lawful money of Canada (the "**Loan**" or the "**Principal**"), and this Agreement will be evidence of the indebtedness of the Borrower to the Lender, and such indebtedness shall include the Loan and all interest and fees accrued thereto pursuant to this Agreement (the "**Indebtedness**").

**Section 2: Interest**

The Loan shall bear simple interest at an annual rate equal to 12%, payable monthly in arrears, from September 2nd 2015 (the "**Borrowing Rate**").

**Section 3: Term**

The entire outstanding Loan and all interest thereon shall become due and will be payable by the Borrower to the Lender at the Lender's address stated above (or at such other place as the Lender may from time to time designate by notice in writing to the Borrower) on September 2nd 2017 (the "**Maturity Date**"), unless the Indebtedness under this Agreement is prepaid in whole pursuant to Section 6 of this Agreement.

**Section 4: Set-up Fee**

The Borrower agrees to pay the Lender a $131.25 set-up fee (the "**Set-Up Fee**").

**Section 5: Monthly Payments**

A. During the term of the Loan, the Borrower will pay the Lender a minimum of $250 per month via Interac e-Transfer to @ gmail.com (the "Monthly Payment"). The Monthly Payment will be applied in the following order:

1. Interest
2. Fees
3. Principal

B. The Borrower agrees to pay the Lender the Monthly Payment on the 3rd day of each month (the "**Due Date**"), starting on October 3rd 2015.

**Section 6: Prepayment**

At any time after the Effective Date, the Borrower may prepay the Indebtedness in whole or in part without penalty.

**Section 7: Representations and Warranties of the Borrower**

The Borrower hereby represents and warrants to the Lender, acknowledging and confirming that the Lender is relying on such representations and warranties without independent inquiry in entering into this Loan Agreement and advancing any funds hereunder, that the Borrower has the legal capacity and right to enter into this Loan Agreement to which it is a party and do all acts and things and execute and deliver all agreements, documents and instruments as are required thereunder to be done, observed or performed by it in accordance with the terms and conditions thereof.

**Section 8: Transfer, Successors and Assigns**

The terms and conditions of this Agreement shall enure to the benefit of and be binding upon the respective successors and assigns of the Borrower. The Lender may assign, pledge, or otherwise transfer this Agreement without the prior consent of the Borrower. This Agreement may be transferred only upon surrender of the original Agreement, accompanied by a duly executed written instrument of transfer in form satisfactory to the Borrower and the transferee.

**Section 9: Governing Law**

This Loan Agreement and all acts and transactions pursuant hereto and the rights and obligations of the parties hereto shall be governed, construed and interpreted in accordance with the laws of the Province of British Columbia, without giving effect to principles of conflicts of law, and the parties will attorn themselves to the jurisdiction of the courts in the City of .

**Section 10: Notices and Documentation**

Any notice required or permitted by this Agreement shall be in writing and shall be deemed sufficient upon delivery, when delivered personally or by a nationally-recognized delivery service (such as FedEx or UPS), or 48 hours after being deposited in the Canadian mail, as certified or registered mail, with postage prepaid, addressed to the party to be notified at such party's address as set forth on the first page of this Agreement or as subsequently modified by written notice.

**Section 11: Amendments and Waivers**

Any term of this Agreement may be amended only with the written consent of the Borrower and the Lender. Any amendment or waiver effected in accordance with this Section shall be binding upon the Borrower, the Lender, and each transferee of the Agreement.

## Section 12: Criminal Code Compliance

In this Section, the terms "interest", "criminal rate" and "credit advanced" have the meanings ascribed to them in s. 347 of the Criminal Code (Canada) as amended from time to time. The Borrower and the Lender agree that, notwithstanding any agreement to the contrary, no interest on the credit advanced by the Lender under this Agreement will be payable in excess of that permitted under the laws of Canada. If the effective rate of interest, calculated in accordance with generally accepted actuarial ice rinks and principles, would exceed the criminal rate on the credit advanced, then:

(a) the elements of return which fall within the term "interest" shall be reduced to the extent necessary to eliminate such excess;

(b) any remaining excess that has been paid will be credited towards prepayment of the Loan; and

(c) any overpayment that may remain after such crediting will be returned forthwith to the Borrower upon demand;

and, in the event of dispute, a Fellow of the Canadian Institute of Actuaries appointed by the Lender shall perform the relevant calculations and determine the reductions, modifications and credits necessary to effect the foregoing and the same will be conclusive and binding on the parties.

## Section 13: Reimbursement of Out of Pocket Expenses

The Borrower shall reimburse the reasonable legal fees, professional fees, disbursements, out of pocket costs (including any applicable taxes thereon), fees associated with bank drafts, cashiers' cheques, mail, collection and demand letters, non-sufficient funds, wire transfers and email money transfers, incurred by or for the account of the Lender in connection with the transactions contemplated herein. The Lender may deduct such costs incurred directly from any advances under the Loan.

The Borrower shall also reimburse the reasonable legal fees, professional fees, disbursements and out of pocket costs (including any applicable taxes thereon) fees associated with bank drafts, cashiers' cheques, mail, collection and demand letters, non-sufficient funds, wire transfers and email money transfers incurred by or for the account of the Lender in connection with enforcing any of the Lender's rights under this Agreement or any of the other transaction documents contemplated under this Agreement.

## Section 14: Recall of Loan

The Lender may immediately recall the Loan and demand full repayment of all outstanding interest, fees and principal if the Borrower fails to satisfy any terms or conditions in this Agreement. The Borrower shall repay the Indebtedness within 30 days of receiving this demand.

## Section 15: Acknowledgement of Risk

The Borrower acknowledges and understands that there are serious legal and financial risks associated with entering into this Agreement. The Borrower's failure to satisfy any of the terms or conditions stated herein may result in (but are not limited to) legal action and the involvement of collections agencies. The Borrower further acknowledges and understands that failure to satisfy any of the terms or conditions herein may impact its future ability to borrow or receive credit from any entity. (Borrower's initials)

## Section 16: Independent Legal Advice

The Borrower and the Lender acknowledge and agree that each party has had the opportunity to seek independent legal advice with respect to the subject matter of this Agreement.

The Borrower acknowledges and agrees that it has sought independent legal advice or waives such advice (Borrower's initial)

## Section 17: Counterpart Execution

This Agreement may be executed in counterpart and delivered via electronic email in scanned document format and together such counterparts shall be deemed to constitute a single original.

## Section 18: Severability

The provisions of this Agreement are severable. In the event of the unenforceability or invalidity of any one or more of the terms, covenants, conditions or provisions of this Agreement under applicable law, such unenforceability or invalidity shall not render any of the other terms, covenants, conditions or provisions hereof unenforceable or invalid; and the Parties agree that this Agreement shall be construed as if such an unenforceable or invalid term, covenant or condition was never contained herein.

**Section 19: Currency**

All references in this Agreement to "dollars" or "$" are to Canadian dollars.

**Section 20: Waiver**

The waiver by either party of any breach of any provision of this Agreement shall not be construed as a waiver of any subsequent breach.

**Section 21: Headings**

The headings in this Agreement are for convenience and reference only and shall not affect the interpretation of this Agreement or be construed in any way as additions to or limitations of the covenants and agreements contained herein.

**Section 22: Entire Agreement**

This Agreement constitutes the entire agreement between the Borrower and the Lender, and supersedes all prior agreements and understandings, oral or written, by and between the Borrower and the Lender with respect to the subject matter hereof.

[EXECUTION PAGE FOLLOWS]

IN WITNESS WHEREOF, the parties have caused this Agreement to be executed under seal of the day and year first above written.

ASSADI

Signature:

Name: ALEXIS SHAHRIAR ASSADI

Title: Director

Witness for the Lender:

Name:

Address:

Signature:

LTD.

Signature:

Name:

Title: Director

Witness for the Borrower:

Name:

Address:

Signature:

EXHIBIT D

# LETTER OF GUARANTEE

**LETTER OF GUARANTEE**

TO: ASSADI (the "**Lender**")

FROM: (the "**Guarantor**")

DATE: August th 2015

**1.** In consideration of the Lender dealing with **LTD.** (the "**Borrower**"), the undersigned and each of them, if more than one, hereby jointly and severally guarantee payment to the Lender of all present and future debts and liabilities (direct or indirect, absolute or contingent, matured or otherwise), now or at any time and from time to time hereafter due or owing to the Lender whether incurred by the Borrower alone or jointly with any corporation, person or persons, or otherwise, including all costs and disbursements incurred by the Lender in view of recovering or attempting to recover those debts and liabilities.

**2.** In this guarantee, the word "Guarantor" shall mean the undersigned, and if there is more than one, it shall mean each of them.

**3.** This guarantee shall not be affected by the death or loss or diminution of capacity of the Borrower or of the Guarantor or by any change in the name of the Borrower in the membership of the firm of the Borrower through the death or retirement of one or more partners or the introduction of one or more other partners or otherwise, or by the acquisition of the business of the Borrower by a corporation, firm, or person, or by any change in the objects, capital structure, or constitution of the Borrower, or by the Borrower or the business of the Borrower being amalgamated with a firm or corporation but shall, notwithstanding the happening of any such event, continue to exist and apply to the full extent as if that event has not happened. The Guarantor agrees to monitor changes in the financial position of the Borrower and hereby releases the Lender from any liability resulting therefrom.

**4.** All monies, advances, renewals, and credits in fact borrowed or obtained from the Lender shall be deemed to form part of the debts and liabilities, notwithstanding any lack or limitation of status or of power, incapacity, or disability of the Borrower or of the directors, partners, or agents thereof, or that the Borrower may not be a legal or suable entity, or any irregularity, defect, or informality in the borrowing or obtaining of such monies, advances, renewals, or credits, the whole whether known to the Lender or not; and any sum that may not be recoverable from the Guarantor on the footing of a guarantee shall be recoverable from the Guarantor as sole and principal debtor in respect thereof and shall be paid to the Lender on demand with interest and accessories as herein provided.

**5.** This guarantee shall continue and be enforceable notwithstanding any amalgamation of the Lender with any other corporations and any further amalgamation, in which event this guarantee shall also extend to all debts and liabilities then or thereafter owed by the Borrower to the amalgamated corporation. Furthermore, all security, real or personal, moveable or immoveable, that has been or will be given by the Guarantor for those debts and liabilities shall be valid in the hands of the Lender, as well as its successors and assigns.

**6.** It is further agreed that this shall be a continuing guarantee, and shall cover and secure any ultimate balance owing to the Lender.

**7.** This guarantee shall bind the Guarantor together with his or her heirs, successors, executors, administrators, legal representatives, and assigns until termination thereof by notice in writing to the manager of the branch of the Lender at which the account of the Borrower is kept, but such termination by any of the guarantors or their respective heirs, successors, executors, administrators, legal representatives, or assigns shall not prevent the continuance of the liability hereunder of any other guarantor. Such termination shall apply only to those debts or liabilities of the Borrower incurred or arising after reception of the notice by the Lender, but not in respect of any prior debts or liabilities, matured or not. The notice of termination shall have no effect on those debts or liabilities incurred after reception of the notice that will result from express or implied commitments made prior to reception.

**8.** This guarantee will not be diminished or modified on account of any act on the part of the Lender that would prevent subrogation from operating in favour of the Guarantor. It is further agreed that the Lender, without exonerating in whole or in part the Guarantor, may grant time, renewals, extensions, indulgences, releases, and discharges to, may take security from, and give up or release any or part of the security held, may abstain from taking, perfecting, registering, or renewing security or from realizing on security, may accept compositions and otherwise deal with the Borrower and with any other person or persons, including any of the guarantors, and dispose of any security held by the Lender as it may see fit, and that all dividends and monies received by the Lender from the Borrower or from any other person, capable of being applied by the Lender in reduction of the debts and liabilities hereby guaranteed, shall be considered for all purposes as payment in gross which the Lender shall have the right to apply as it may see fit, not being bound by the law of imputation, and the Lender shall be entitled to prove against the estate of the Borrower upon any insolvency or winding up, in respect of the whole debts and liabilities. The Guarantor shall have no right to be subrogated to the Lender until the Lender has received payment in full of its claims against the Borrower with interest and costs.

**9.** If any circumstances arise necessitating the Lender to file its claim against the estate of the Borrower and to value its security, it will be entitled to place such valuation as the Lender may in its discretion see fit, and the filing of such claim and the valuation of its security shall in no way prejudice or restrict its rights against the Guarantor.

**10.** The Lender shall not be obliged to exhaust its recourse against the Borrower or other persons or the security it may hold before being entitled to payment from the Guarantor of each and every one of the debts and liabilities hereby guaranteed, and it shall not be obliged to offer or deliver its security before its whole claim has been paid. The Guarantor waives all benefits of discussion and division.

**11.** All indebtedness and liability, present and future, of the Borrower to the Guarantor are hereby assigned to the Lender and postponed to the present and future debts and liabilities of the Borrower to the Lender. The Guarantor hereby grants to the Lender a security interest in all such indebtedness and liability as security for the performance of the Guarantor's covenants herein and the payment of the present and future debts and liabilities of the Borrower to the Lender. All monies received from the Borrower or on his or her behalf by the Guarantor shall be held as in his or her capacity as agent, mandatary, and trustee for the Lender and shall be paid over to the Lender forthwith. This provision will remain in full force and effect, notwithstanding the termination of the guarantee under the provisions of paragraph 7, in which event it will terminate when the debts and liabilities of the Borrower to the Lender covered by this guarantee under paragraph 7 have been paid in full.

**12.** This guarantee is in addition to and not in substitution for any other guarantee, by whomsoever given, at any time held by the Lender, and without prejudice to any other security by whomsoever given held at any time by the Lender, and the Lender shall be under no obligation to marshall in favour of the Guarantor any such security or any of the funds or assets the Lender may be entitled to receive or have a claim upon.

**13.** The Guarantor shall be bound by any account settled between the Lender and the Borrower and, if no such account has been so settled, any account stated by the Lender shall be accepted by the Guarantor as conclusive evidence of the amount that, at the date of the account so stated, is due by the Borrower to the Lender.

**14.** The Guarantor shall make payment to the Lender of the amount of his liability forthwith after the demand therefore is made in writing. Such demand shall be deemed to have been effectually made when an envelope containing it addressed to the Guarantor at his or her last address known to the Lender is deposited with postage prepaid in the post office. The liability of the Guarantor shall bear interest from the date of such demand at the rate or rates then applicable to the debts and liabilities of the Borrower to the Lender.

**15.** This guarantee and agreement shall be operative and binding upon every signatory thereof, notwithstanding the non-execution thereof by any other proposed signatory or signatories, and possession of this instrument by the Lender shall be conclusive evidence against the Guarantor that this instrument was not delivered in escrow or under any agreement that it should not be effective until any condition has been complied with. None of the parties shall be bound by any representation or promise made by any person relative thereto that is not embodied herein. The liability of the Guarantor hereunder begins on the date of his or her signature on this Letter of Guarantee.

**16.** This guarantee shall be binding upon the undersigned and any of them, if more than one, jointly and severally between them and with the Borrower and also upon the heirs, executors, administrators, and successors of the Guarantor, and will extend to and enure to the benefit of the successors and assigns of the Lender. Each and every provision hereof is severable, and should any provision hereof be illegal or not enforceable for any reason, such illegality or invalidity shall not affect the other provisions hereof, which shall remain in force and be binding on the parties.

**17.** The Guarantor acknowledges having read and taken cognizance of the present Letter of Guarantee before signing it and declares that he or she understands perfectly the terms, conditions, and undertakings contained therein.

**18.** This Letter of Guarantee shall be construed in accordance with the laws of the province of British Columbia and the Guarantor agrees that any legal suit, action, or proceeding arising out of or relating to this Letter of Guarantee may be instituted in the courts of that province and in the city of , and the Guarantor hereby accepts and irrevocably submits to the jurisdiction of those courts, acknowledges their competence, and agrees to be bound by any judgment thereof, provided that nothing herein shall limit the Lender's right to bring proceedings against the Guarantor elsewhere.

IN WITNESS WHEREOF, the parties have caused this Guarantee to be executed under seal of the day and year first above written.

________________________________

Witness Name:

Witness Occupation:

Witness Address:

Witness Signature:

EXHIBIT E

# DIRECTORS' RESOLUTION

Resolution of the Directors of (the "**Corporation**")

Made and passed as of this 3rd day of March, 2014

WHEREAS:

A. It is desirable and in the best interest of the Corporation that Alexis Assadi be granted full signing authority on behalf of the Corporation;

NOW THEREFORE BE IT RESOLVED as a Resolution of the Directors of the Corporation that:

1. Alexis Assadi is hereby granted full signing authority on behalf of the Corporation.

We, the undersigned, being the Directors of the Corporation, hereby consent to the Resolution herein recorded, as evidenced by our signatures set out below.

______________________________

Alexis S. Assadi
Director

______________________________

Director

EXHIBIT F

# NET WORTH STATEMENT

**Net Worth Statement**

Name: ____________________

DOB: ____________________

Address: ____________________

Marital status: ____________________

Personal Income: ____________________

| Assets | | Liabilities | |
|---|---|---|---|
| Cash and term deposits: | | Current Bank or Credit Institution Loans: | |
| Accounts and notes receivable: | | Accounts Payable/ Unpaid Bills: | |
| Commodities: | | Credit Card Debt: | |
| Limited Partnership Investments: | | Co-Signed Loans/ Guarantees: | |
| Vehicles: | | Auto Loans: | |
| Real Estate: | | Mortgages: | |
| Total Assets: | | Total Liabilities: | |

Net Worth: ____________________

## About the Author

Alexis Assadi is an investor, writer, executive, scotch and cigar enthusiast, watcher of comedic videos and animal lover. He has personally financed over 50 small businesses across British Columbia, ranging from health clinics and fitness studios to real estate ventures, wealth management companies and marketing firms.

Visit him at AlexisAssadi.net and subscribe to receive free informational emails.

CPSIA information can be obtained
at www.ICGtesting.com
Printed in the USA
LVOW04s0517230616
493716LV00017BA/77/P